black as i am

ZINDZI MANDELA and
PETER MAGUBANE

foreword: ANDREW YOUNG

The Guild of Tutors Press
1019 Gayley Avenue   Los Angeles, California 90024

copyright © 1978
by zindzi mandela
& peter magubane.
all rights reserved.
except for book
reviews, no part
of this book may
be reproduced
in any manner
except by
permission of
the publisher.
library of congress
no. 77-87417
ISBN no. 0-89615-001-1
made in the usa.

photograph of
peter magubane
by suzette abbott.
edited & designed
by paul o. proehl.
set in helvetica
light.

CONTENTS

A tree was chopped down / 3
Peter Magubane / 6
Zindzi Mandela / 9
Foreword by Andrew Young / 11
Home is where sorrow is born / 12
Gimme just a little bite / 14
Dream of frustration / 16
Savior / 17
If my right hand was black / 18
Lord we are black / 20
Holy baptism / 24
Standing close to time / 26
Ode to my father / 28
Lock the place in your heart / 30
Children / 31
Drink from my empty cup / 36
His unspoken words / 37
The current gone away / 38
The song that life plays / 40
Women / 44
Dry my tears / 48
Suicide came to me / 50
Mother / 52
I felt so depressed / 54
Childhood days / 56
The black bird / 58
A furnace of hands / 60
In a troubled dream / 62
Where are you / 64
Hold my hand / 65

There are families / 66
The night comes out / 68
So you've heard it before / 70
Child / 72
Leaning dangerously / 75
She lay on the tombstone / 76
Why does every pain / 78
Go / 80
Arriving in a cold damp house / 82
I need a neighbor who will live / 84
My mind was blurred / 86
Take my hand / 88
She silenced him / 90
It was dark / 92
The cold wind crept / 94
Sitting, side by side / 96
I waited for you last night / 97
His face a sorrowful sight / 98
My heart was empty / 100
Anger like warm milk / 101
She uses her chief possession / 102
I have tried hard / 104
Curiosity / 106
A forehead creased / 112
There's an unknown river in Soweto / 114
Loneliness / 115
Your rivers of glory / 116
Yes, it is me / 118

Index of titles and first lines / 120

A tree was chopped down
and the fruit was scattered

I cried
because I had lost a family
the trunk, my father
the branches, his support
so much

the fruit, the wife and children
who meant so much to him
tasty
loving as they should be
all on the ground
some out of his reach
in the ground
the roots, happiness
cut off from him.

For Nelson Mandela
in his imprisonment
and for
Nomzamo Mandela
in her sentence
of silence, who
suffer as they do
for all of us.

I am grateful to David Goldblatt, Vita Palastrante and Clive Emdin for having assisted me in my needs, and for the support of Raymond Louw of the *Rand Daily Mail*. I wish also to express my appreciation to Pentax, which mounted the exhibition of Zindzi's poems and my photographs at the Pentax Gallery, Johannesburg.

Peter Magubane

PETER MAGUBANE

For Peter Magubane, a prize-winning photographer for the *Rand Daily Mail,* August 26, 1976 started off as just another working day. It ended in a way that news photographers in other parts of the world would consider cruel, unbelievable, and intolerable.

Magubane is one of several black staff members of the *Daily Mail.* His assignment on August 26 was to go to Soweto, the black African township outside Johannesburg, South Africa, where some 1,000,000 people live. There he was to photograph once again disturbances which had started about two weeks before. No white journalist covered the trouble; none was allowed in the area by government order.

But Peter Magubane never lifted a camera on this particular day. He was taken into custody by the security police before he had an opportunity.

The charge? None was given, nor was any required.

The explanation by police? "The arrest was in connection with Magubane and what he does. We don't arrest people because they work for the *Rand Daily Mail,*" said the Commissioner General of Police.

What does Magubane do? He covers the news with his cameras. For doing what he was supposed to do he was picked up without explanation and hauled off to jail.

What happened to Peter Magubane on August 26 was nothing new to him. Magubane, 43, has been a working newsman in Johannesburg for years. In that time he had other critical confrontations with laws that journalists of the free world must think of as strange to say the least.

On August 10, for example, Magubane went to Alexandra, another black township, to check on unrest there. On this assignment police beat him up, breaking his nose and bruising him severely. Magubane explained what happened:

"We saw policemen hitting and arresting people as they walked along the street. We followed in our car [he was with a reporter] and I took several photographs.

"We reached a roadblock. The police ordered several men to remove it. As they did so, the police hit them with batons and I photographed the incident.

"A policeman rushed towards me with a rifle. I pleaded with him not to hit me. Another policeman joined him and began to hit me with a baton.

"They took me to a colonel who told me I had no right to take photographs in an operational area."

The colonel then ordered Magubane to remove the film from his camera and expose it. He was forced to do so under repeated baton blows. This was not Magubane's first beating at the hands of police. Only the week before he was assaulted by police while on assignment in Soweto.

Physical assault is not the only means used by police in South Africa to discourage Peter Magubane and other journalists. An even more effective weapon is arrest under internal security laws that permit indefinite detention without habeas corpus.

In 1969 Magubane was arrested and held in solitary confinement in a jail in Pretoria for 586 days. During this time he twice was acquitted of charges but afterwards returned to solitary. There he did not have even reading matter. When, eventually, he was released, he was banned for five years. A ban in South Africa for all practical purposes forbids social or business intercourse, puts severe geographic limits on the travel of the person who is banned and, of course, prevents a journalist from pursuing his profession. He was released from ban in October, 1975, after five wasted years, and returned to work at the *Daily Mail*. In 1976 he was again detained, this time for 123 days.

Peter Magubane started taking pictures as a schoolboy with an old box camera. Someone had given his father the camera on his rounds as a fruit vender in Sophiatown. The young photographer sold his snapshots for a shilling and sixpence. He left high school to take a job in the photo department of *Drum* magazine, first as a driver and then in the darkroom. Then came his first picture assignment. "I made a success of it," he said, "and since then I have never looked back."

He won his first awards in 1951. In 1962 a British photo magazine rated him one of the best ten cameramen in the Commonwealth. By 1971 he had won fourteen international awards and his work had appeared in such well-known publications as *Life*. In 1967 he joined the *Rand Daily Mail*. His first detention by South African security police came two years later.

In 1976, Magubane won the South African equivalent of the Pulitzer Prize—the Stellenbosch Farmer's Winery Award for Enterprising Journalism—and the Nick Tomlinson Award in the United Kingdom for his coverage of the Soweto and Alexandra riots.

The pictures in this book are of the slums which lie on the outskirts of Cape Town and Johannesburg. They were put on exhibition along with Zindzi's poems at the Pentax Gallery in Johannesburg in 1977 under the title "Shanty-towns."

There is grimness, sadness and even the terror of poverty in these pictures and in these poems. But there is also happiness and love. Can there really be happiness in these places? Magubane was asked.

"Yes, there is a lot of happiness. You see, if you are happy, you tend to forget the grimness. People are not happy because they are living there. But life has to go on, and they have their happy periods."

Hatred after his experiences? "My experiences with the police have not changed my outlook. I have no hatred and do not intend hating."

This is Peter Magubane's first book, as it is also Zindzi Mandela's. We are privileged to publish it. We look forward to presenting soon *Black and Fourteen* by Zindzi Mandela, a group of her earlier poems, and Magubane's *Riot at Soweto: This Is My Body, This Is My Blood.*

The pictures that accompany Zindzi's poetry are not to be taken as literal expositions of each poem. Each art form stands on its own. The photographs of Magubane establish the setting and create the mood in which the warm, poignant and powerful poetry of Zindzi Mandela gains even greater depth and intensity.

Paragraphs one through fifteen of this biography of Mr. Magubane are from an editorial written by Robert E. Gilka, Director of Photography, the National Geographic Society, which appeared in *News Photographer*, December, 1976. The remaining paragraphs are from an article on Mr. Magubane, "A Slice of Life", which appeared in *focus*, official organ of the S.A. Pentax Gallery, Winter, 1977. We are grateful to Mr. Gilka, to Mr. William Kuykendall, Editor of *News Photographer*, and to *focus* for permission to reprint.

ZINDZI MANDELA

When Nobutho Zindziswa Mandela was born on December 23, 1960, her father Nelson was already "banned" by South African authorities. A banned person is under a sort of house arrest under such severe restrictions that he or she becomes almost a "non-person." When Zindzi was eight weeks old, her father was forced to go underground. In 1962 he was arrested and in 1964 began serving a sentence of life imprisonment on Robben Island, the notorious maximum security prison off Cape Town. Zindzi knows her father from photographs, his writings, and his reputation.

Within two years of Zindzi's birth, her mother, Nkosikazi Nobandle Nomzamo Mandela, was also banned because of her activities as a national executive member of the Federation of South African Women.

It was a difficult and precarious childhood from the beginning. Just before Zindzi was born, her father learned that his son, Makgatho, was ill in the Transkei, possibly of tuberculosis. Mr. Mandela went to get him without asking permission, as required by law. In his absence Zindzi was born. Returning to Johannesburg, he went to the black hospital where Zindzi and her mother were, and found Zindzi — only two days old — suffering from diarrhea. He took mother and child and stormed out of the hospital (since closed because it was in an area declared to be "white"). Two months later, when her husband went underground, Mrs. Mandela had to go to work to supply the family with food. Both Zindzi and her sister, Zenani, were cared for by relatives. They never had their own family life.

Zindzi was placed in a nursery, which had an excellent "mother" and reputation, but Zindzi rebelled. At the age of four she told her mother that "I am a big girl and the others are babies. I won't go to the creche (nursery)." Her uncle once tried to bribe her with barbecued chicken, but without success. Zindzi simply said, "Keep your chicken."

Zeni, then five, was then attending school in a convent in Kliptown, the closest school using English, and so Zindzi was allowed to toddle along. But this was a school for "coloured" (of mixed races) and Zeni and Zindzi were required to leave. Similarly, at the City and Suburban School, also for "coloured," the principal was threatened by security police for admitting the little girls. They then entered a school in which instruction was in Afrikaans. Although this was a strange language to them, both passed the year's final examination. In all their various schooling experiences, Mrs. Mandela was never able to meet any of her girls' teachers — under her ban, she could not visit the schools!

In 1967, Zindzi entered "Our Lady of Sorrows" school in Swaziland. The school was appropriately named for the experiences Zindzi underwent there. Happily, Sir Robert and Lady Elinor Birley then entered the lives of Zindzi and Zeni and took over their education. Lady Elinor and her husband were at Witwatersrand University on an exchange program. When Lady Elinor met Mrs. Mandela and learned of her distress over her daughters' education, Lady Elinor offered to help. Under these auspices little Zindzi started writing poetry, using it to vent her anger and frustration at her educational experiences and her religious instruction. This persistent questioning is apparent in her writing today: How does Christianity relate to the plight of the black man?

We are told Zindzi was an affectionate and generous child — and this capacity for love and compassion is also obvious in her poetry. But it went beyond sharing the family's food with neighborhood children: she used the side of their house as a blackboard to teach her playmates English words and arithmetic. Zindzi could also be stubborn and tough. She asserted herself. Once at mealtime she told her mother, "Mum, if I say I do not want cabbage in my food, I do not want it, like big people do not want certain things. You do not want porridge because it makes you fat, and we children do not force you to have it."

The Birleys arranged for Zindzi and Zeni to enter Waterford School in Swaziland. Here Zindzi excelled in sports and drama, and her poetry blossomed. She was encouraged and helped by her English master, Michael Linden, and his wife, and when the Lindens left, by Ronnie Chamber. It was Uncle Ron who provided consolation and guidance in Zindzi's "brooding moods" when she thought of her parents, her lack of home life, the artificiality of school life, and the complications of being black.
Zindzi matured very early in her life. She left Waterford last year after winning high marks and a prize for her poetry.

This is the crucible — the family, the community, the nation, the longing, the oppression, the love, the agony — in which the poetry of Zindzi Mandela is fired and from which it flows.

It is the voice of a young woman of South Africa which must and will be heard. *Listen!*

FOREWORD

It is still possible as a tourist to visit South Africa, to wine and to dine, to dim one's eyes and to leave without seeing what Zindzi Mandela sees. It is still possible to feel the breezes off the Cape or the warm sun glowing off the rolling hills and not to feel what Zindzi Mandela feels. What is not possible, however, is to look into the eyes of a black man in South Africa and not to understand where Zindzi Mandela is. Her poems are a mirror of those eyes—of the eyes of a child of Soweto, of a young mother waiting in a line for non-whites, of a black laborer with sweat glistening on his back. They are eyes full of questions. They are eyes that can light with mirth and laughter and never quite lose the shadow of pain. They are eyes that can hold love and friendship as well as quiet rage.

The South Africa that Zindzi Mandela is and feels, and that Peter Magubane has captured so well in his photographs, is a land on the edge of a consciousness whose time has come, and whose power dwarfs that of police and armies. It is the consciousness of the fundamental dignity of all of us, brothers and sisters under a Creator, and of the fundamental birthright of our freedom.

The black child that Zindzi describes who "has enough worries to burden the world . . . and make it crack" is in the vanguard of that consciousness. It is he who will combine the suffering of his parents with growing pride in his own black being-ness to shape the forces for change. It will be his questioning of injustice that will bring justice. It will be his rage over the indignities imposed upon him that creates a new society recognizing the dignity of every spirit. Zindzi and Peter show us not just people —but a process unfolding which confirms yet another time the intrinsic truth, in all races and in all centuries, that to be born is to be free. Their contribution to that process in these pages is both sensitive and profound.

Andrew Young
New York, October 14, 1977

Home is where sorrow

   is born

Home is a place to return to

   that provides a roof

nothing valuable beneath

   for the black man

Home that accommodates

   a frustrated wife

   emancipated parents

   deprived children

   dependent relatives

Home the living grave

   the burial

Oh, to be black!

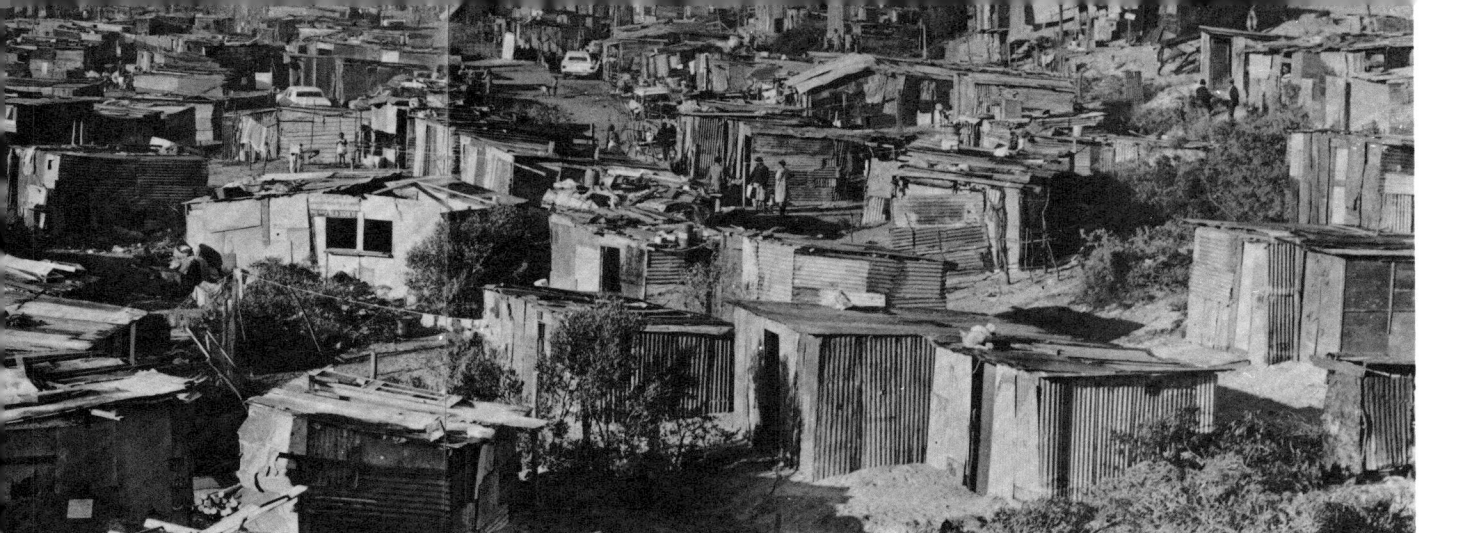

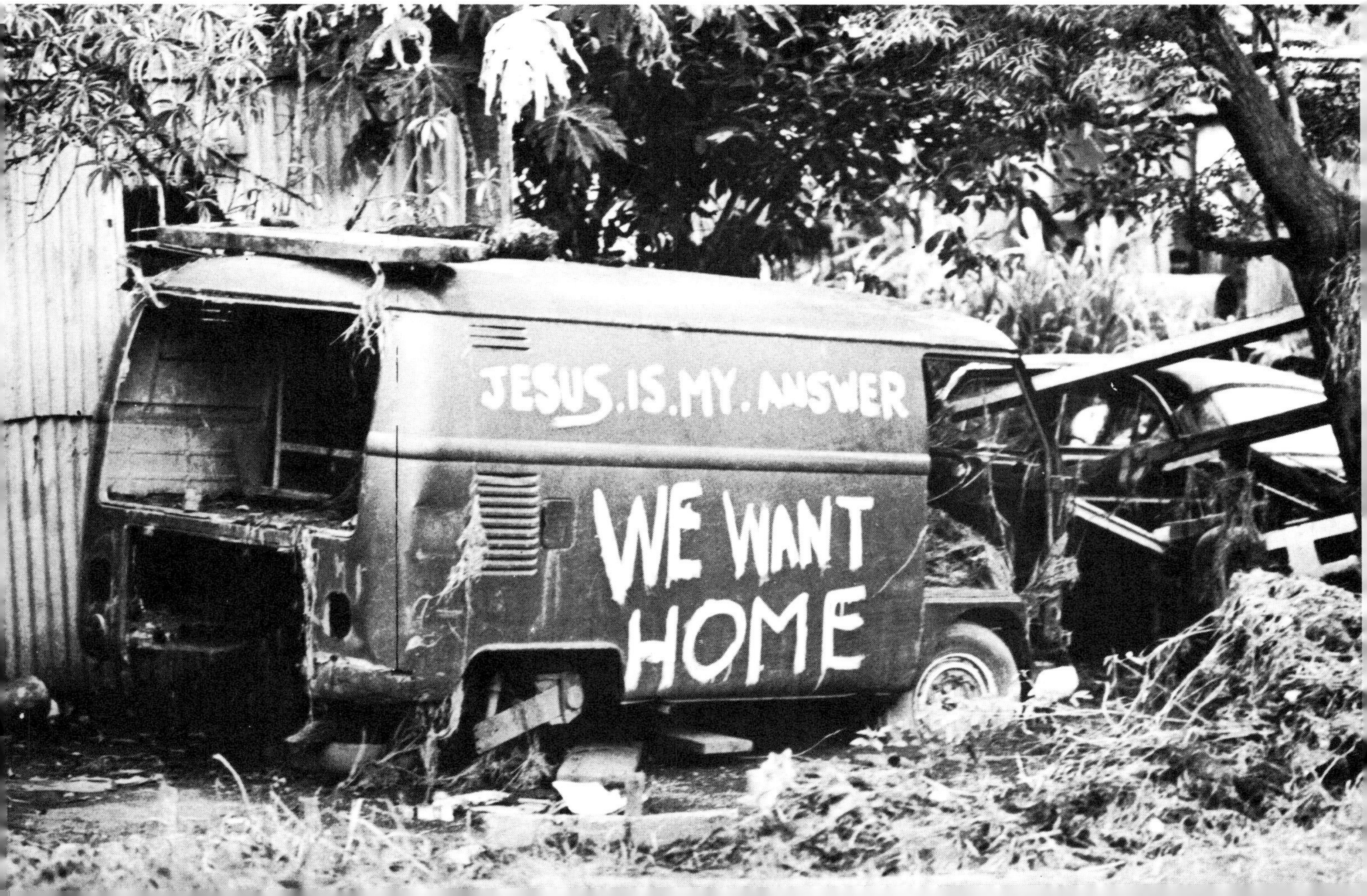
JESUS.IS.MY.ANSWER
WE WANT
HOME

Gimme just a little bite

of your baked love

please

    just a bite

Gimme just a little sip

of your overflowing pride

please

    just a sip

Gimme just a little lick

of your melting desire

please

    just a lick

Gimme just a little taste

of your appertising joy

please

    just a taste

Gimme just a little meal

of your attractive being

please

    just a meal

Dream of frustration

In my dream

an old black woman stirs

and

seeing the tears run down my cheeks

slowly

sips them

    for life

then

wakes me up

anxious to face dawn

I touch her

    to know if she's alive

but in my living

an old black woman dies

Saviour

An old woman standing

a young daughter opposite

both are waiting

in a wrinkled mind

    where are you Lord?

in a blossoming mind

    what are you Lord?

a white child running

a black child kneeling

both are young

in a polished mind

    a prayer tonight

in a deprived mind

    kneel all and sundry

an old man dying

a young son watching

both are pensive

in a dimming mind

    into your arms Lord

in a sorrowful mind

    release these chains

If my right hand was white
and my left hand was black
they would only meet in prayer

because

they would not both be in one pocket
at the same time:
it would be too uncomfortable.

Why

do both exist on the same body
if it is painful
when they are together?

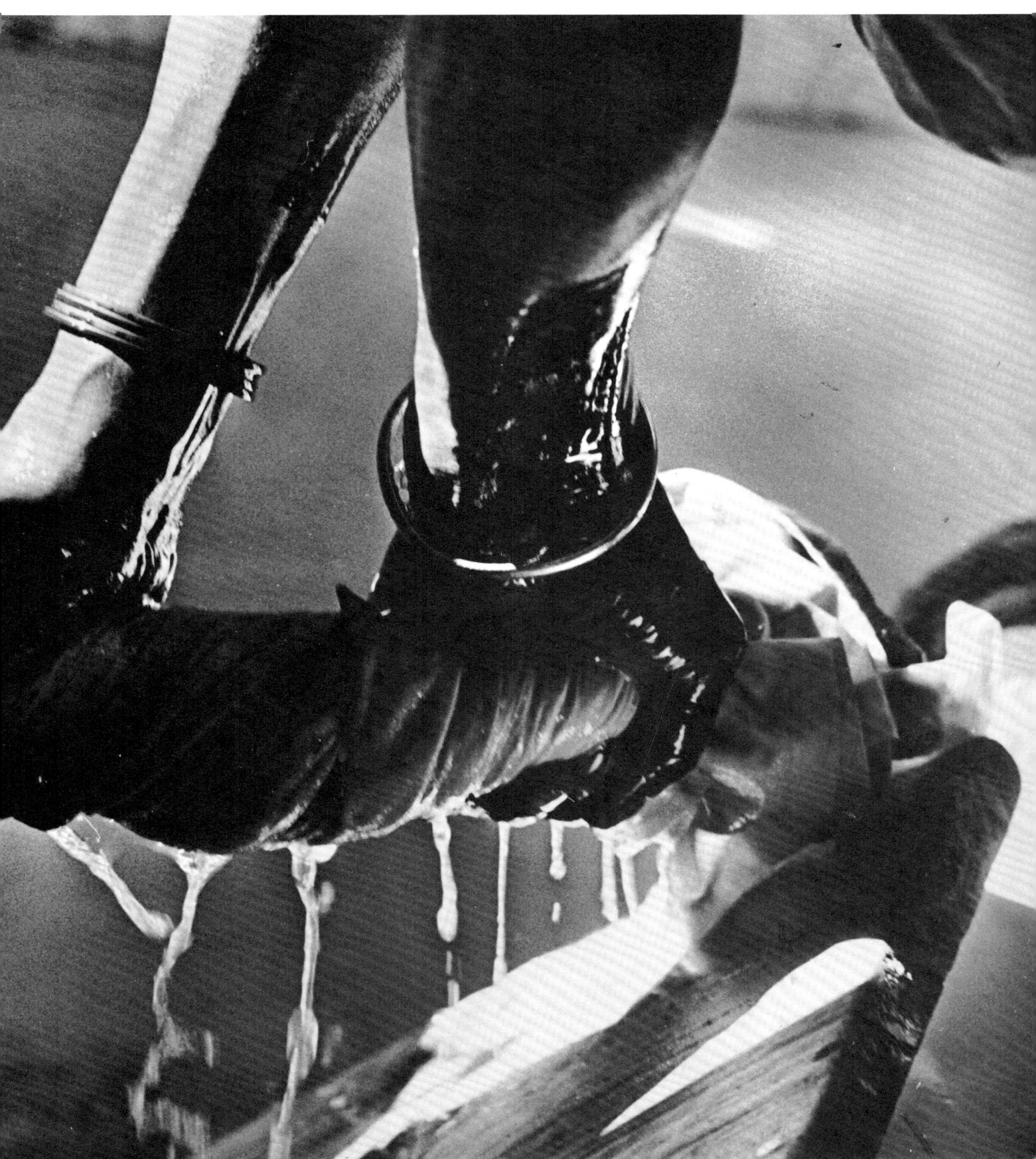

Lord

we are black

even in prayer

because

when we do worship

we are silenced

by the white man

who lent you to us

We do not need a roof anymore

to protect us

and to bring us closer to you

If all our leaders have gone

then you have to lead us

and show us the way

a tunnel to freedom

is our prayer

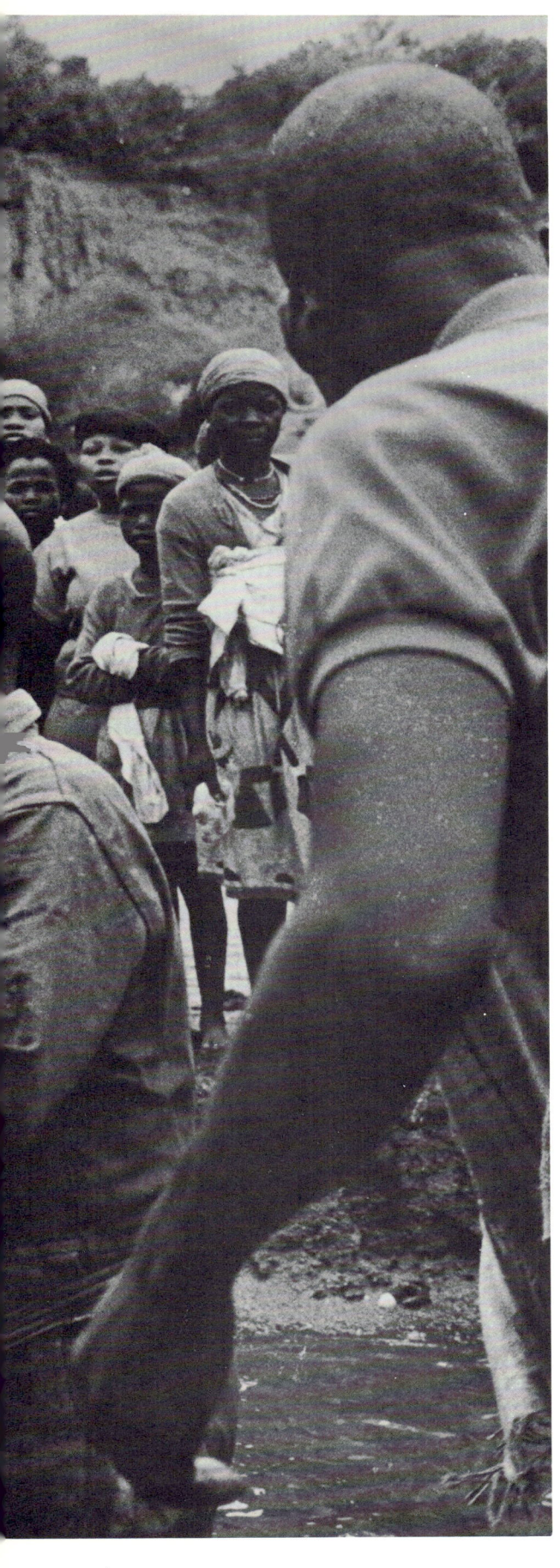

Holy baptism

O so cleansing

    purity

    innocence

    satisfaction

    encouragement

    light

but darkness

when not properly done

but sorrow

when not done

Then

let me see my God

guide me

because I cannot

    on my own

Standing close to time

leaning against yesterdays

thinking about the present

learning to love

learning to hate

learning

through experience

not school

dying

through fighting

not natural causes

saying baas

to a junior

being a boy or girl

even when fully grown

the black child

alone

has enough worries

to burden the world

and make it crack

Ode to My Father

Tata

I can imagine

    what you would be

    if I was not

    what you would say

    if I kept quiet

I can imagine

    where you would go

    if I remained

    where you would end

    if I started

I can imagine

    what you would admire

    if I was disgusted

    what you would love

    if I only hated

I can imagine

    when you would die

    if I lived

    when you would cry

    if I laughed

I can imagine

    what you would enjoy

    if I felt depressed

    what you would do

    if I did not

Lock the place in your heart

into which I have poured my emotions

I do not want to be hurt again

use your heartbeat as the key

only you can hear if it unlocks itself

If the wind around you

should blow away

breathe into it and let my secrets go

Children

I saw as a child

a small white boy

sitting in a car

and I never knew why

when my home was so far

and his so near

I had to walk

I saw as a child

a tall building

beautiful and empty

and I never knew why

when my home was so small

and this so big

we were overcrowded

I saw as a child

a tarred road

clean and lonely

and I never knew why

when our street was so busy

and this so alone

it was uncared for

Drink from my empty cup

and be proud

that nothing could quench your thirst

the reality

satisfied you

likewise

be hungry

crave for food

tremble at the sight of beer

kill

and feel free

then know

that you are so oppressed

you even laugh at yourself

his unspoken words

clasped tightly

in the curve of my smile

he loves

deep in my thoughts

pounding nearer to his eye

flowing and fresh

cooling my flushed tear

unconscious above me

he whispers

low in my pulse

kissing

lightly against his lip

soothing and soft

caressing my weeping body

we love

tearing in our separation

a hollow

painted in passion

The current gone away

to cry on to the bank opposite

soil dissolving with sympathy

ripples forming like

flowing tears

mine

as I remember

a home so far away

there is no bridge

to take me there

but a wet world

    of obstacles

The song that life plays

is the joy that children bring

like a new melody

on a rusty guitar

flowing into your ears

hypnotising your mind

creating

relaxation like a drug

growing from moisture

your blood

into an addict like love

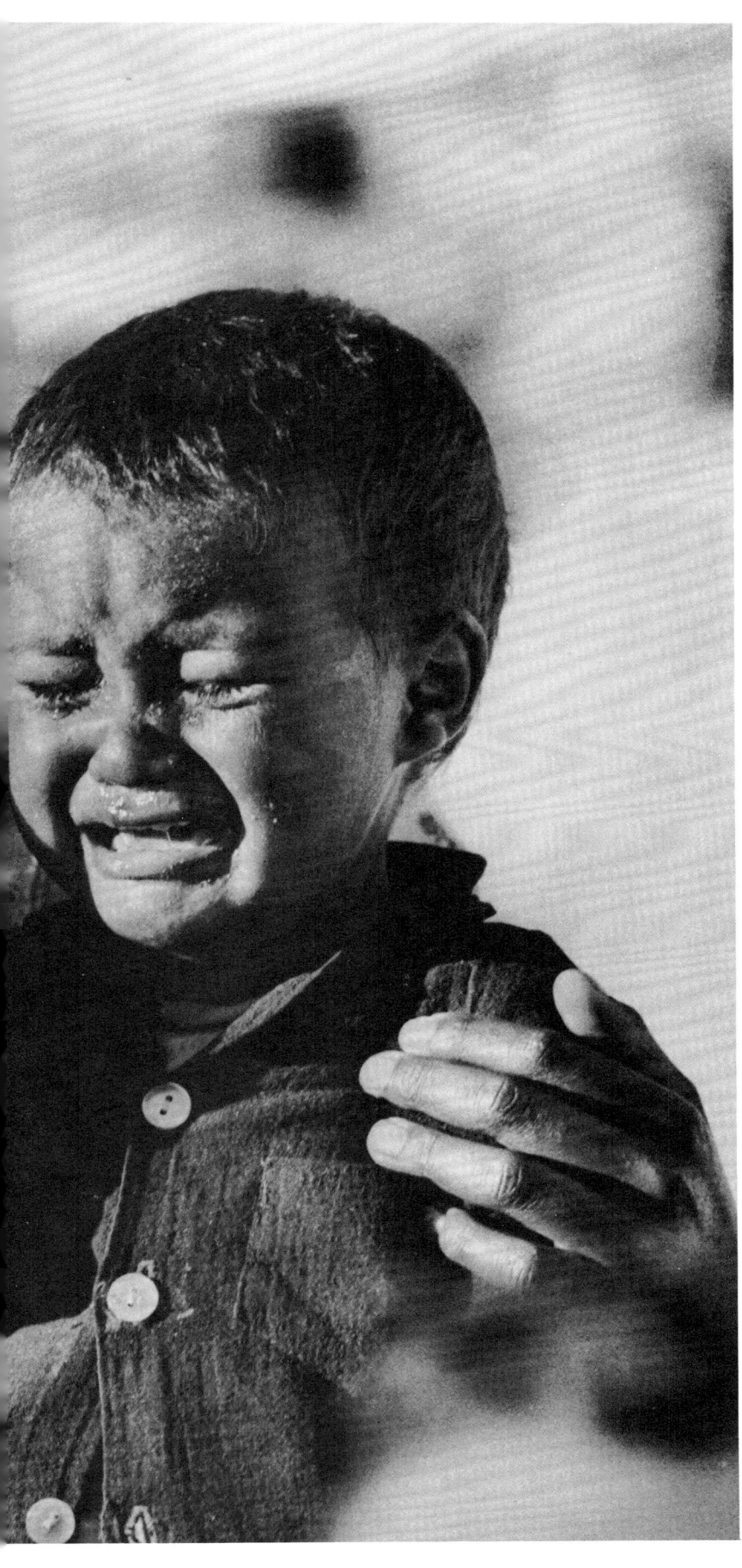

Women

My life is but a dirty penny

that is only valued because

it is the only one

My life is but a ten rand note

that can be used only because

there may be change

My life is but a faithful husband

who smiles alone only because

he thinks he knows

My life is but a broken mirror

that still stands up only because

it has to act

Dry my tears

O, pain of comfort

and

emphasize

the lazy crowd

melting in our brotherhood

hold my hand

and lead me

back to my birth of happiness

and make me understand

the impossible

O, iron out

these wrinkles of sorrow

drain them dry

let them be

a desert of relief

and shut my mouth

because every breath I take

pollutes my dammed waters

and ignites them

to vigorous flows

into the hollows of my eyes

because they could not

    understand me

and I, them

so I kept my distance

they would not

leave me alone

Suicide came to me

like my mother on a cold day

in her arms like a nest

weeping like a stormy sky

my death like an old building

I had been demolished

I lay in ruins

Mother

hands so black

veins so apparent

like snakes on a mirror

Mother

face so greasy

wrinkles so deep

like roots embedded in soggy ground

Mother

heart so sore

breasts so dry

like a brown valley and a rocky hill

Mother

body so still

cheeks so cold

like a frozen statue

I felt so depressed

O terribly

and all I could do was cry

but

where were you mama

I felt so lonely

O terribly

and all I could do was go

but

where were you mama

I felt so thirsty

O terribly

and all I could do was swallow

but

where were you mama?

Childhood days

    far away

Slipping through my aging fingers

falling into my sweetest memories

so hot

    that steam evaporates

and

the drops dissolve

in the cold forgotten air

I always cry

when

I think of my happiness   so far

its innocence   that I wish I could reach out

    and confidence   and bring them back

in my childhood days   knowing

    far away   that I won't let them go

         no

             not again

The black bird

perched itself on the cement world

as it jerked its little head

and faced me

I saw the white patch on its chin

and

before I could study it further

    it took off   then

leaving me the admirer   her tail a dot far away

and the wall the support   bids me farewell

waiting   all I can do is smile

every morning she comes   and wipe the tears off my face

to display herself   awaiting

for a few minutes   again

insults the wall   that black bird

by her little gift droppings   my beauty

gives me her back   who reminds me

and takes off gracefully   of myself

    gliding at an odd angle

A furnace of hands

releases a flame

that cries out

    its origin

and dissolves

in the warm air above it

slowly

    drops

        drop

onto the furnace of hands

releasing steam

that cries out

    burning

and dissolves

in the warm air above it

now

the furnace of hands

    no heat

is spoiled

In a troubled dream

I see two grey hands

    in a black atmosphere

one hand beckons

the other

    repels

the beckoning hand disappears

reappears

with a teardrop in the palm

beckoning

    beckoning

        beckoning

the other

    tenses

the beckoning hand disappears

reappears

with a cut on the wrist

beckoning

    beckoning

        beckoning

the other

    is still

the beckoning hand disappears

reappears

beckoning

        moving towards the other

the other

clasps the beckoning hand

and raises it higher

than itself

Where are you

    are you

        you

            echoes a fading voice

Strangled in a thought

of a love-sick mind

calling

calling

calling

a voice that whispers

with a perfumed breath

I can't go on

  can't go on

    go on

      on

Where are you darling

are you turning in your bed

are you trembling absent-minded

are you walking endlessly

are you shaking your head

because

if you aren't

darling I am

and thinking about you

again

again

again

Hold my hand

    I'm afraid

only through tiny spots of light

your face

    comes from behind a dark robe

of blackness

kiss my brow

    I'm numb

only with passion

I tremble

    life from a broken cup

grows again

rub my back

    I'm in pain

only your hands of feather touch

soothe me

    bathing a frozen body

with warmth

love my memory

    I'm dead

only when you live

only when you find me elsewhere

only when you forget me

only then

    will I gently

tug at the rope

    around your neck

There are families

who are so happy

they never shed a tear

so

the many times they weep

are

the few times

that they use

to think about others

There are the families

who are so rich

they never give a penny

so

the many times they starve

are

the few times

that they ever use

to feed others

There are the families

who are so oppressed

they never know the reason why

so

the many times they understand

are

the few times

that they are ever given

to forget that black is sin

The night comes out

    and we all wait

shivering

    like lonely blades of grass

we all cry out in

    gutteral spasms

our minds are clogged

    with stale blood

we smelled of fresh vomit

    and bile

the dawn never came

    only a tornado

the environment dissolved

    into nothingness

a consolation

    that we were together . . . alive.

So you've heard it before

We are inhumanely treated

We are hidden from all

So you've heard it before

We die of starvation

We die of frustration

So you've heard it before

We live on liquor

We live on blood

So you've heard it before

So I've complained before

So we've heard

    you liberated

    our fighters

and so we've failed before

Child

Child

you were born

into a warm world

of white

    sterilized coats

you were made to cry

you were held

against my swollen breasts

you cried

your tears

never fell onto your cheeks

you broke

inside me

you kissed my neck

when you didn't stop the days

from going away

Child

you were born

without a father

but

you were happy

you played with my thoughts

Child

you stared at

    and saw

a raindrop

laughing with you

you let

a sharp-toothed rat

eat

the centre of your palm

and died

Child

  you drank the dew

  that slept til morning

  on a rose petal

  and you loved it

  and the years

  went by and by

and

child

you did too

when

you passed me in the yard

walking

like God

had first kissed you

on your forehead

I looked back

and heard a baby cry

I saw blood

I smelt a nurse

I felt pain

then relief

in my womanhood

  Child

  child

  changing child

My child

rocking in a chair

smoking a pipe

brushing a kitten

My child sightless eyes

facial expressions

of crushed white paper

My child

watching you child

from a covered grave

you above me

crying

    and

praying

trying to dry your face

but

your hand is motionless

with age

trembling at your side

Oh child

my child

looking around you

making love to the

    setting sun

with your silken soul

Child

I am washed of you

you are not in my coffin

I am dusty with dust

you are dusty with ash

blowing from within

you were on fire

your tears put it out

you cremated yourself

    child . . .

Leaning dangerously

    over a bridge

I saw you as the water

and I wanted to kiss you

    with my body

and loved only the hatred in me

you had thrown pride over your shoulder

at me

    searching

    searching

there I was

I had looked everywhere.

She lay on the tombstone

crucified by her father's spirit

guilt cut through her

like a fish in water

he had called her name

his hand had reached out for hers

his misty eyes had searched

the ceiling above wildly

and had accepted death

she had been walking

the streets all night

for customers . . . for money

to take her father to the hospital

the man had cancer

    who knew?

she sold herself for a rand

    who knew?

what did the world know

about this burden?

it was a troubled world

    who knew?

Why does every pain

have to be hurting?

Why does every tear

have to be shed?

Why does every joke

have to be amusing?

Why does every scream

have to be piercing?

Why does every question

have to be asked?

Why does every silence have to be echoed?

Why does every tree

have to be climbed?

Why does every sea

have to be sailed?

Why does every road

have to be crossed?

Why does every course

have to be completed?

Why does every whisper have to be controlled?

Go

I said to myself

and do not turn back

they will be waiting for you

you will be welcomed

go . . . go . . . go . . . go . .

I thought:

consolation

Hurry

I said to myself

and do not slow down

they will be patient with you

you will be accepted

hurry . . . hurry . . . hurry . . . hurry

I thought:

contradiction

Laugh

I said to myself

and do not be discouraged

they will be amused like you

you will be one

laugh . . . laugh . . . laugh . . . laugh

I thought:

apprehension

Arriving in a cold damp house

only to find

a melting ice cube

glittering in the moonlight

Losing an only ill child

only to find

a crushed tablet

dusty in the moonlight

Hating a close friend

only to love

a hypocrite

grinning in the moonlight

Entering a dark scary room

only to find

an old lamp

creaking in the moonlight

I need a neighbor who will live

    a teardrop away

who will open up when I knock

    late at night

I need a lover who will sleep

    a touch away

who will hold me

    when I shiver, crying beside him

I need a child who will play

    a smile away

who will always whisper I love you

    be my mummy

I need a shadow that will be

    a breath away

that will console me when it's dark

    go when day breaks

My mind was blurred

and my vision heavy

My thoughts so pale

and my cheeks confused

My mouth no longer heard

and my ears could only whisper

My hands were pounding

but my heart could still write

My stomach walked on

and my legs were hungry

I accepted my muddy fate

Take my hand

for it is still warm

lean on my shoulder

for it is still comfortable

hold on to my apron

for it is still useful

sit on my lap

for it is still soft

step on my foot

for it is still fit

come . . . . .

Take my love

for it is still pink

lean on my pride

for it is still strong

hold on to my generosity

for it is still open

sit on my understanding

for it is still balanced

step on my fragility

for it is still weak

come. . . . .

She silenced him

      by clutching him to her bosom

and thought it would be cruel

to say

I don't know where

      your father is

This child

thought the world

was just mummy

      and

         daddy

Later in life

      he would risk his life

for a stale crust

      of bread

he would kill a man

for being a boy

Now he was asleep

in his mother's arms

preparing for

      a different kind of life

It was dark

the man was drunk

he tripped over a dead body

in a Soweto street

from the church

came wailing sounds

of a hymn being sung

from the mountain

came terrifying screams

of a girl being raped

he got home

and there was no food

the children were shivering

the wife was exhausted   his son had been stabbed

the police came   the girlfriend arrested

he went to sleep

and woke up at 3:00 a.m.

his life was routine

and he felt chained

The cold wind crept

over the foggy horizon

chilling and beautifying

the frozen atmosphere

but the couple walked on

step in, step out

admiring and occupying

its inner fullness

the sun crept over

dazzling in power

making all love present, stronger.

Sitting, side by side

knowing, without hearing

that love was the occasion

feeling, without touching

the girl the boy

her thoughts, loving

the possessiveness held in his eyes

the passion breathed from his nose

the current carried in his kiss

the immaculacy bathed in his neck

what would she do

without this man

he fascinated her

as they sat there

at the riverside

living

a

flowing

life!

I waited for you last night

I lay there in my bed

like a plucked rose

its falling petals my tears

the sound that my room

   inhaled

   drew in softly

   swallowed

in my ears

was the tapping on the window

getting up

I opened it

and a moth flew in

powdering my neck

shrugging

I caught its tiny wings

and kissed it

I climbed back into bed

with it

and left it to flutter around my head

I waited for you last night

His face a sorrowful sight

as he said that

nobody cared for him

His shoulders a stooping clay figure

as he said that

he was hopeless

His chest a heaving volcano

as he said that

he was exhausted

His ribs a protruding rack

as he said that

nobody gave him food

His stomach a rumbling vacuum

as he said that

he was thirsty

His legs a bony dishrag

as he said that

he felt aged

His feet a wet torn mass

as he said that

he was lost

His luggage an empty basket

as he said that

he sought charity

His frame a silhouetted skeleton

as we know

he would always be remembered

My heart was empty

but I was very grateful

and in that hollow silence

in which I was a vacuum

my thoughts were like raindrops

floating in my heartbeat

Anger like warm milk

burned and caused a smell

on my mind like a stove

ablaze with my conscience

my hands were like withered roses

trembling against my temples

She uses her chief possession

this black woman

to satisfy her baby

this black woman

She uses her chief possession

this black woman

to make him grow

this black woman

to seduce 'baas'

this black woman

She uses her chief possession

this black woman

to make money

this black woman

She uses her chief possession

this black woman

She uses her chief possession

this black woman

as a suffering mother

this black woman.

I have tried hard

brother

and I won't give up

even if

that which I cannot see

creeps up behind me

and crushes me to pulp

or even if

that which I cannot see

overtakes me

and leaves me behind

to ponder

      conclude

I have yet to take

another step

and within that time

develop

Curiosity

She put her dizzy head

into the scratching soil

and was so happy

she laughed at the sun

but the grass died

like time

she crept through the night

and was so confident

she laughed at the moon

but danger was born

she held out a small hand

and cupped a fallen raindrop

and was so generous

she laughed at the clouds

but heat was drier

like age she climbed up a tree

and was so aware

she laughed at the ground

but the branch lowered

she trod on to broken glass

and felt new pain

and was so betrayed

she laughed at the blood

but the tears fell

like destiny she hid in a corner

and was so afraid

she laughed at the darkness

but death was alight

A forehead creased

to emphasize the pain

Eyes wet

to empty the grief

A mouth tightened

to keep control

Black clothes

to weigh down the sorrow

and then we ask you

if you are there

or

why me

or

Lord do you really understand

or do we?

There's an unknown river in Soweto

some say it flows with blood

others say it flows with tears

a leader says

it flows with health and purity

the kind of water

that nobody drinks in Soweto

There's an unknown tree in Soweto

some say it bears sorrow

others say it bears death

a leader says

it bears health and purity

the kind of fruit

that nobody tastes in Soweto

There's an unknown river in Soweto

there's an unknown tree in Soweto

the body

the blood

both unknown

Loneliness

was the name of the game.

death

the score

His emotions and inner turmoil

were cards laid out on a table

He gambled himself

He owed himself

the life he never had

He was bankrupt of quality

TRUTH

CHARITY

DESTINATION

Your rivers of glory

have overflooded many banks

Your streams of mercy

have rippled upon dead souls

Your waters of truth are no more

Your stems of living

have dug out many plants

Your branches of giving

have stolen many fruit leaves

Your trees of charity are no more

    every twist of a branch

    is the road to changes

    for me and for you

    but when we reach

    our destination

    we cannot go back

    or straighten the path

    we just dangle

    on the sharp edge.

Yes, it is me

and in spite

of life's ups and downs

I will live on

eternally

and leave my dust

on every rough path

with each stone

marking my every inspiration

my every breath

my every existence

and each step I take

I will walk quicker

and dissolve in my environment

and appear in space

as a solitary anthem

sung by every voice

swelling with sound

and rising to a crescendo

of my visions and thoughts

Yes, it is me

Study me carefully

tear me and rip me apart

turn me inside out

unfold my mysteries

digest my realities

soothe my deep pains

drown in my matured eyes

and find yourself

in the darkness surrounding me

INDEX OF TITLES AND FIRST LINES

A forehead creased / 112
A furnace of hands / 60
A tree was chopped down / 3
Anger like warm milk / 101
Arriving in a cold damp house / 82
Child / 72
Childhood days / 56
Children / 31
Curiosity / 106
Dream of frustration / 16
Drink from my empty cup / 36
Dry my tears / 48
Gimme just a little bite / 14
Go / 80
His face a sorrowful sight / 98
His unspoken words / 37
Hold my hand / 65
Holy baptism / 24
Home is where sorrow is born / 12
I felt so depressed / 54
If my right hand was black / 18
I have tried hard / 104
In a troubled dream / 62
I need a neighbor who will live / 84
It was dark / 92
I waited for you last night / 97
Leaning dangerously / 75
Lock the place in your heart / 30

Loneliness / 115
Lord we are black / 20
My heart was empty / 100
My mind was blurred / 86
Mother / 52
Ode to my father / 28
Savior / 17
She lay on the tombstone / 76
She silenced him / 90
She uses her chief possession / 102
Sitting, side by side / 96
So you've heard it before / 70
Standing close to time / 26
Suicide came to me / 50
Take my hand / 88
The black bird / 58
The cold wind crept / 94
The current gone away / 38
The night comes out / 68
There are families / 66
There's an unknown river in Soweto / 114
The song that life plays / 40
Where are you / 64
Why does every pain / 78
Women / 44
Yes, it is me / 118
Your rivers of glory / 116